CHICKEN ON CHURCH

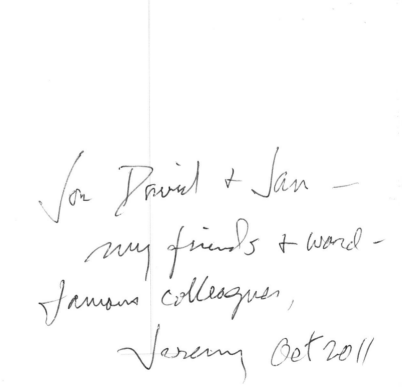

For David + Jan —
my friends + word-
famous colleagues,
Jeremy Oct 2011

CHICKEN ON CHURCH

AND OTHER POEMS

JEREMY LARNER

BIG ROOSTER PRESS — 2006

To order online
bigroosterpress.com

Big Rooster Press
Box 1012
Lafayette, CA 94549

bigroosterpress.com

jeremylarner.com

ISBN 0-9773618-0-2

Book and cover design by Steven Zahavi Schwartz
meantimespress.com

Cover photgraph © 199? by Lars Topelmann
Background photos by Jesse Larner
Author photographs by Susanne Kaspar

CD recorded 2005 at Riegerworld Studios, Berkeley, CA
Engineered by John Rieger

CONTENTS

CHICKEN ON CHURCH

For Hal Sampson
For John Solomon
For Paul Willen

CHICKEN ON CHURCH

Sing to me, why not?
O ancient & overloaded island,
the song of one lone chicken,
or rumble it in your wall-like roar,
muffled among prophecies
more improbable than even
a giant rooster, our feathered
wanderer and survivor,
who struts your streets in style,
never lost though often clueless
as to where he's going, ready
at every instant to deal with
epochal urban obstacles,
delays and inconveniences, never
squawking or needing to fly
to the heights of lofty display,
at his ease in the mix of people
ever moving, speaking, jostling,
leaving behind them detritus
of constant invention, yes,

life's garbage, foul, fowl, sweet &
smelling like a barnyard rose! I yield
to you, O great and dangerous city,
center of my universe, hear me as
I hear you for one last day's ramble,
stay with me, focus my distracted
inner eye, furnish as always the new
or illuminate the all-time true, let
the song of the chicken warble
full and in tune long after my voice
remains only in echoes of empty
airshaft whispers... Lead this driven
and unlikely traveler to the hollow
thumping depths, as I follow your story
southward & down, backwards
like a home-bound hero halfway
through life's journey led down
into the underworld, safe at last
& sure as I would be could I slip back
into the womb from which I came...
or the many wombs before it.

Down where the dangling island
narrows, the two rivers angle & merge,
cut off the land we first landed on,
down on cracked brick streets where
storehouses in the age of industry
swept the world's cargo off the wharves,
train-tracking it West out
into the body of America, where
settlers nailed new lives with anything
effort could buy & space
without end never enough
wide deep broad enough territory
for what they raised, grew, built,
ate, burned & threw away, nor time
to stop in a new world so raw
that to stop is to die, to cease
to buy & sell is to turn bottom up
and rot by the side of the trail.
Here Canal Street got its name
from a stream of westward-winding sewage,
where now it teems with awninged
storefronts booths & stalls, as
we shoulder through jangling tribes

of shoppers from far as Far Rockaway
or Dover, diving through heaps of
re-wrapped phones, flawed gems, & fresh
digital quartz, digging into piles of ersatz
fashion jerseys label for label
twins of fine designer junk,
coolie-copied in secret cellar sweatshops,
below the alleys & avenues where
bargain-seekers flip through bins
of oyster rolex ripoffs & thumb the knobs
of Korean chronometers, thick as clams,
—& if they like, duck
into sexshops to inspect grime-boxed
cellophaned cassettes and multiple
oriface dolls, big as life when inflated,
just like you & me, male & female
socket wrenches line the pathway
to the Holland tunnel, plus stolen
CD decks & packs of perfume,
essence of Europe's desperate armpit
refinement, while seatcovers
of every known synthetic beast
sit stacked for sale

alongside blaster shops where
noise-collectors come on weekends
to wedge four-foot boombox
sub-woofers into trunks & beneath
backseats of maniac machines,
the auto-embodiment
of urban bald or hairy manly
pride growling & grumping
round the block, not caring
if they blast the brains
of toddler-dragging nannies
or case-clutching suits ambling
up from Wall Street to lunch
at filmstar gourmanderies,
see & be seen, then score
furtive drugs from dealers lurking
each to his holding zone beneath
scaffolding girdling windowless
radar-topped phone company towers,
bee-hived with cells of gibbering
phantics linked from here to Bangalore
and trained to wig out customers
who call with query or complaint,

trigger instant profile scans
beamed to circling satellites,
so that all citizens endowed
by their creditors with inalienable
debts are driven nuts by the humming
of hidden charges, heard or imagined,
non-negotiable, soon to accrue
to a trigger-point setting off
a speed-of-light laser to flash your data
to all the world's crooked collectors,
exponentially compound
your interest & repossess your frozen assets,
your mass consumer plastic
to be seized & instantly invalidated
the very next time you dare to slip or
slide your card in the free-trade universe!

Yet all this while down on Church Street,
the drive for one-of-a-kind personal pleasure
lives & thrives, as still solvent stubbornly
sexual furtive city guys draw twenties

from cash machines and venture
off their sidewalk safety and into
the warm by winter steaming hot
by summer cave of Harmony Heaven,
haven of old-time burlesque,
even now providing & parading all
we hold primal. Down the steps
between the bouncers & through the
beaded curtain, deep into the vault
of this dark den, men
of all ages, stages & incomes
happily tumble & hopefully
peep up along the outskirts of
a shabby stripper's runway rubbed
to the nubbin by B-girls' bottoms
as semi-dancing bon-bons
slide close & open wide
the knees, if you please,
for the delectation of front-row
connoisseurs, while
down in the dim arena,
strumpets wander
in languid underwear, gliding

through fields of eyeballs, passing
their parts like canapes, yes,
for any mother's son who pulls
a crinkly picture of a President,
the wanton of choice seats herself
navel to navel, trollop to tummy
in her customer's lap &
grinds her quim like grandfather's
trusty Swiss-HongKongian timepiece,
jiving & moaning maybe at your
ribald whispers & maneuvers, or,
for older dudes who play the dad,
our hired siren confides the lost job
at the teller's cage, the kids
left back in the apartment,
the bills & illness, the dream
of night law school or
start-up cash for simulated
shrimp farm, never missing
a bump or sigh, her semi-fondling
not without comfort for the lonely
of heart, the tender of loin, & if
the shrimp be sweet & halfway clean,

his nurse for the nonce may kiss
for a quid his speechless lips, hey,
in this age of scary sex you
can't have here, she will lay
his weary head on her bare bodkin,
let him graze or feed or fondly pluck
whatever within limits just might
substitute for the true, real
substitute satisfaction,
measured in the privacy
of his very own pants, reckoned
against the unstoppable, sequential tick
of seconds zipping by sixty
to the minute, as the dainty lady
lifts loose bills with
fingers deft & cruel as
time itself, the deal is done
& money run to dust... & outside down
on Church Street we must keep on,
like time itself, come finally
to America, even here,
o stout-legged pioneers,
stand-ins or stand-downs

for a people, they say, who
brought the Bible westward,
to keep the Word as it were,
as He kept His Word & rested only
on the seventh day after finishing
Salt Lake City. South of Canal,
where pieces of the street itself
give way to ancient rot & crumble,
we must totter, pilgrims, into the past
and out again, stumbling ever on,
the stars our destiny!
past the old post office
with bold depression murals from
a time when artists got paid to work
and who could afford culture?
—let alone sell the description
as the thing itself, along with
the T-shirt—and downward!
we continue, boats against
the current, beating backwards
against a tide of noontime
trial attendants, jury panels,
even a high judge incognito

(as ultimate judgment must be,
hidden, holy, secret as birth control),
past glassed-in ranks & rows
of phone-booth fossils,
wrecked & abandoned
in the age of cell to cell
instantaneosity, while human units,
never alone except always,
walk through nowhere, software plugged
to ear-socket, drowning in static,
yelling to holographic ghosts,
ignoring the battered phonebooths
upright like troops at the last review,
enscrolled in soldierly graffiti
from head to foot, formal
as a Pharaoh's coffin-lid....

Our footsteps subtly clatter,
sinking into cobblestoned sidestreets
along West Broadway now, where we
glimpse the minaret of a hidden mosque

& pieces of the Statue of Liberty,
her spiked crown peeping
from a rooftop garden or
her welcoming hand hoisting
high and holding tight the torch,
& in a dusty alley we slip beneath
an overhead passageway, arching
like the Bridge of Sighs
behind the Venice cathedral,
where rivals of the doge were led
from prison cell to execution chamber,
though here in the New World we are
every one of us escapees, seeking
each his true disguise, *our dream*
they say on talkshows, *don't let*
anyone take it, hang on to
that sales slip, your guarantee
of life, liberty, and a brand new
blue-eyed soul! —rebirth of all kinds
available but sorry no refunds,
all sales sooner or later final!
…as trailed by our shadows & speckled
in flecks of sun & shade we pass by

warehouses of wornout wholesalers,
lofts of urban art freelancers,
one wild parrot shop & a 12-inch
burrito bar, buy one, take one
in your mouth and bite down tight,
as at last we find
a cozy trattoria
sitting within a tar-patched shell
of a cracked & crumbling
concrete-columned two-story fortress,
like a succulent Sicilian gnocci
in a wine-dark Aegean sauce.

Fronting our Roman palace,
along the Church Street curb where
the immortal chicken will soon set
webbed foot into my saga,
a testimony of noontime limos sit,
as impeccable gangsters or
politicians or slumming insiders
seeking retro mob-boss flash

lounge at leisure within and eat
discretely luscious lunches,
sheltered from prying eyes
in backbooths where they carve
who is to shake down what
from where & sort out civic prizes,
honors & titles, later
to be mentioned at wakes &
well-watched burials, the honors
due all big-time urban deaths,
no matter if the well-fed capo bursts
from a lifetime's stuffing,
or buys a bullet in business
as he knows it, he knows at least
he will not die of heartbreak.
Let the lamblike bumpkin fresh
from the sticks smelling
of sheepdip & brimming
with barnyard bromides yearn
for lost causes & noble poverty,
the life of the scholar & artist
he dreamed while riding Old Bossie
through prairie mists—on his way

to the Big Town, hoping himself
one of the storied few, who come
even now across the sea or from the farm,
from the stockyards, the South
or the rocky West or the blue-skied
middle cities bringing what deserves
to last in every generation, and
after getting lost & taken to the edge
of losing faith, they triumph,
so it's said, alive or long dead—
none of this matters
to the prince of the city with price
of admission tucked in his ex-
crocodile belt with microchip pager &
personal side-arms according to
god-given might-makes-right,
he eats that hayseed's dream
for lunch with his *osso bucco* ,
ensconced in daily deference,
the rustproof warranty of power,
his place in the pecking order
to take or not take, as he wishes,
whatever is there to take, no

fishwrap Phoebus even makes
his radar screen, though the boy or girl
who toothbrushes his tablecloth
may be Shakespeare or Sarah
Bernhardt. How could he know
that yes, on that very block,
as on all others of the lower island,
in the offhand smartness of the street,
the glory of New York goes by,
each one alone yet available,
unaware of rank or title,
perk or pride or well-placed pals,
the dues he's paid, the lunches due him
—or who he's told he is
on TV's tuned to focus groups!
that jazz dissolved with every step
along the sidewalks of the real,
among passersby who pass by power
not needing or caring
or knowing to submit. Here,
if anywhere, pass free women
beyond class, caste, price or pre-fab
costume from mooning moron

magazines, at home among
the men who walk the world
with offhand inner amusement, sure
to catch your drift or the pith
of your crack, just so! deep
to the inmost inside layer,
where doubt revolves through
exaggeration and plunks
like an 8-ball into synchronicity's
side-pocket! Look & listen,
friend & buddy, find
souls at home here, taking it
for granted or struggling
to be born, each tuned
to its own odd inner scale, yet
able to follow the figures
of the urban fugue,
and from the corner of the eye
without colliding or missing
a word or a step, pick up
the passing world
dissect & dismiss it,
adding one's own note

to the would-be symphony
of give & take, accretion
of urban exactitude, changing
with the changes or sometimes
not, the only choice to risk it
on the sidewalk or else
suffocate in uptown swank or
crash & burn or simply stall
on the world's foul freeways.
Citizens of the lower island,
pledged to live & die there,
speak as they choose & in
the flash of a synapse take
your measure & top
your wisecrack, not even
trying or looking up
from the horse page or the market
or the sandwich they make you
or the laundry the register
the all-day book or the next trick
bopping through the door, each
undefined and indefinable. Forget
income, in-group, brand-name

fame, in true New York we
greet each man & woman
just the same. Out there,
at last, once more, out there!
where the world is most alive,
each may choose to serve,
but sorry, not to sell the soul
or be sold, unlike, say,
the twinkery of tabloid stardom
on the passing newsracks or
the cavalry of chauffeurdom,
waiting all this time with fuck-all faces,
zoned-out & grim as Marines
in jungle outposts who
lean their jodphorbottoms
on glossy fenders or lay back
in soundproof tinted depths
where waves of tone-tweaked
twelve-speaker air-cooled
lunchtime limo music
break upon the pulled-down
officers' dress-caps covering
their twitching dozing faces.

....All this, in all its daily changing,
almost the same as always,
my incubation years before
the chicken came my way
so long ago who cares
how long since last I was here,
the 23 years since I left or
the 33 since I first came fierce young
& easily-excited, unable
to make my deal & deal with it,
my nagging worry inaccessible
as a sore tooth, plagued with
hangover immigrant
jitters, nightsweats of oldworld
terror & grinding immobility,
shades of old New York, where
the already too-old parents
of my parents stayed at first, crushed
among nervous & excited greenhorns,
not a mile from where I walk now,
free to be sick & poor, sink

or swim or get their children
swimming lessons
in the deep blue unfathomable
American sea, across whose surface
we sail with whatever wind,
no shore in sight and hearts
a-thump with hope & fear,
because read all about it,
the amazing truth is
nothing yet is settled, and....

Here I come again, breezing along
on my daily democratic
sidewalk shuffle, a one-time one-
of-a-kind hero-in-his-own-mind
hot-shooting left-handed nose-hair
out of backwoods Indiana,
escaped once more from cookie-box
streets, beehive canyons, cardboard
climbers & cloistered killer cubbyholes
of hollyhood... to find myself

alive once more in sheer relief
of urban lostness, no need for
pettiness or pride, praise or blame,
loose at last, leaving behind
a lifetime's bootless fussing,
to wander the wilds of Manhattan,
accepting the worldly mix
with mixed to heavy irony...
   when what do I see but A CHICKEN!
a six-foot sad skinny feather-suited bird
lounging between two limos gazing
balefully into traffic edging North
on Church Street. A San Francisco clown,
I think, but why the glum stare,
the shy head-tuck, is the bird blue
because stroller-shoving mommas,
finger-popping garment-stackers, thesbians,
lesbians, salesmen & fabric-buyers,
buttoned junk bond brokers, invisible
among innumerable murmuring variations
of the hip or sodden unemployed,
keep on keeping on

their noon-break errands or
cluster on frescoed slab steps,
without a blink in his direction?
I stop I grin to let my frere my
fellow wanderer, bird impersonator,
groundbound skylark, my outcast
downcast roostermanchild
see himself observed & appreciated,
but hey!
he scrapes his rubber-clawed foot
cocks his floppy-wattled head
on his pitiful scrawny neck
in obvious chicken-snit irritation.
He vants like Garbo to be alone
in the big city, and true enough,
this gink encased in outward show
of featherhood could walk
from the Battery to the veldt
of Van Cortland Park
paradoxically cocooned
from cool gothamite curiosity,
which would hardly stoop

to acknowledge a giant chicken,
nor be provoked to pursue
whatever foul mood depresses
his wishbone. So set apart
is he, so unapproachable
in his chickeninity, he could
stand guard for Mafia diners within,
scanning the street for a flash
of rival conspiracy, or—if
double-yolked to treachery—
on hearing the family signal,
the cosa nostra cock-a-doodle-doo,
enter in egglike innocence
the trattoria, catch
offguard mob chiefs
downing sweetbreads or garlic
eggplanted lamb chops or
excruciating tenderness of veal,
and blast them off this lower
island earth! If need be,
my sullen cock could slouch
uptown, enter the U.N. to drop off
drugs in diplomatic pouches,

enjoy the brusque politique
of Kissinger cunningly confiding
strategic mega-death & famine
in the men's room, then,
for sex-break, saunter past
epauletted Park Avenue doormen
who take no notice as he slips
like a slice of Christmas white meat
into hot penthouse boudoirs
of cloistered concubines.
How gauche of me to think
my chicken-man needs recognition, how
Hollywood to wigwag, Daddy,
I see your thing, I dig it! How
cool the hippest of chickens
to reject the rube's forced fellowship,
no way he'll serve as daily special
on anyone's turista menu,
sit pan fried, rendered &
reduced with onions,
he is a bird who eats not
one who's eaten, neither a fryer
nor a broiler be, my boy, this bird's

a free-ranger with feathers to pluck,
worms to pull & hens to tread!
Traces of pterodactyl perambulate
his chromosomes, mapping evolution
ancient as buried cities, millenia
of mystery migrations,
uptown & down & back in time
to the Babylonian bottleneck
through which the human species
squeezed & intermingled, escaping,
returning, flourishing, trading wares
& work & genes and sudden
as a slingshot getting driven out again!
The chicken smoothes his jaunty tail-plumes,
he's preening, starting to strut, ready
for lift-off, down to do the deal
he dressed for, and as he hops
off the curb he drops a butt
to the gutter as mighty Zeus
once dropped the neck of Leda,
not caring that his spawn
of half-God half-mad beauties

driven by Hera into jealous frenzy
would chop down Troy, most awesome
early onset of all too many
too-tall doomed topless-towered
megalopoli,
the swan's last burning seed bursting
into Queen Clytemnestra,
mean & cunning as a coke dealer,
who, coveting the whole of Argos,
cuckolded Agamemnon
while he was out trashing Troy,
and when her weary warrior
came home to his connubial bed & bath,
the Queen—pricked on by buzzing
harpies—sleeved her sleek royal knife
in the chinks of his majesty's snow
white freshly dis-armored ribcage,
emitting wails of existential glee,
carving her King like a chinese chicken,
cursing like a cabin cook & crooning
queenly hymns of pride & gore as
once more palace walls ran bloody

in assassination's nasty asininity....
  —Officer, Officer, arrest that chicken!
I tell you I trailed him
from Tribeca, saw his yellow-beaked
Kalashnikov crow thunderbolts,
saw burning roosts, roast gizzards,
hacked coxcombs, empty eggs
and ravished pullets!
  —Beat it, bum, before your pervert lies
crack and scramble flocks of decent
families! In Zeus we trust, our
downy chickies' ears must never
hear your wimpy squawking!

Foully rebuffed & in disarray,
I wobble Eastward muttering,
something unKosher on the shores
of Little Italy. My eye is seized
by strangled shapes, brown glazed
ducks dangling head-hooked in windows

of Dim Sum dives, warnings
to would-be Marlowes like myself.
—Forget it, Jake, it's Chinatown,
don't ask what's in it, scarf it down!
Just then a silver Honda beetles
to the curb and the Chicken
flutters into it, bagging himself
for delivery merging upstream
and gone. Only by chance—
or is it classic fate?—
do I spot the Big Broaster
5 hours later at happytime,
hosting a hostile child's show
on the all-cartoon channel,
between cliff crashes shotgun
dissolvings electric frazzlings
& fuse-bomb obliterations,
pitching sugar cereal to catatonic
kidbrains in pre-dinner funk, pacified
while modish Mommy mixes
martinis in time to revive for
after-dinner late night all night

prime time in the Big Apple,
where who knows who
will strut the streets seen
or unseen born or reborn
in the superheated tripleply
green garbagebag of my
homegrown midwestern milkfed
imagination, where anything
may spring from rot & ripen,
burst into bloom?

—And all because
I never could eat food reviews, dress
my restless bod in slick-page images,
zip each night to the in spots,
skimming my own town like a tourist,
squeeze neat chopped thoughtlets
into culture kits or catalogues,
into menu-mags where my name
is one of many appetizers

for diners to slice up, fork me
for their passing pleasure like
one more jerked chicken-thigh
at the latest secret bunkered
hot loud high-priced bistro disco,
fenced by velvet rope and shaved-head
idiots, lords of all the lesser idiots
they keep from trampling in.
What I came back for why
I see me once more flickering
in New York shopfront reflections,
threading the crush and gone,
recalls that one & only Chicken
who came my way on Church but
sorry, no costume no Zeus help us
statement stance or spinoff, what
drove me off the block &
out of town twenty years ago
in shock of sober youth's awakening
was my deep-prized fear & outrage,
arrogance you say & near-fatal
ignorance, still I could not learn

to smell in solemn assembly
of merry-go-rounding clowns
on wooden horses chasing
uptown carrots ever in the way
of my otherwise easy
jaywalking, sounding
their solemn honk through every channel,
to homo sapiens stupified each night,
via worldwide cannibal TV—

> *Here it is, guys n girls n*
> *would-be with-its, your one*
> *& only one last chance,*
> *one network, one spotlight, one*
> *big-tent circus, one*
> *all-inclusive sideshow, one*
> *god or set of gods to be named*
> *at a later date, one*
> *change of costume, one seat*
> *with your name, one*
> *chance in a million you may*
> *already be (!)*
> *the calvinistically karmic*
> *pre-determined all-time onetime*

winner! no waiting, act now!
your face to replace
reality, your word, your whim
the tabloids of the law,
you are inside for good,
star of stars, your headshot
on high, larger
than life, life itself now
you & only you!
your nail-scrapings, your split ends,
our holy relics of the here & now,
your deep thoughts & desires
for world peace inspire
& require, all money is yours,
tax-free, all cars, all girls
are yours, boys too, just play
or seem to play the game,
exposure counts, but
don't stand up, hang on
to your dream! bless the lord &
your mom & just do it,
snatch it, sniff it, scratch it, grab
with effortless ease

your ticket, your entry
to the one & one only
only game in town,
the only town, the big top town
we run (we always will),
all entries mortal and remain
your body & soul our property
—and All right, I say, sorry!
it's not that I don't I just can't,
why bother, why come indoors why
join the lip-synched singsong
of the graveyard-whistling dead,
when life's streaming in
on every breeze from the dappled river,
rushing through every loosened crack,
down every airshaft up every alley,
twisting through tunnels beneath us,
popping off manhole covers
and whipping quark particles
through short hairs of myriad
subway-stair pubic glimpses,
each one ethno-multiply
bristling & tumescent for any shade

of love or wit reflected
in the twinkle of an eye, the only
sign of life there is... & Here
the living souls come,
unseen but all around us,
never so many anywhere!
shaking bouncing cracking
the once-firm sidewalks lining
the bottoms of blue-sky canyons,
each soul effortlessly turning,
gliding to its inner samba,
dancing upside outside inside
its singular self-abnegation,
baptized in immolation of
the emolumizing metropolitan flow.
Now tell me if you can,
how can I leave this scene how
can I step from the stream,
fly West once more as it
keeps on keeping on
rolling on without me?
Let me hang in here
to the end with whatever

ease or illusion of ease
or supple simulacrum
of style & grace, even
as my arteries clog &
my once-deerlike ankles swell
& feet plod cow-plopping that once
danced through wildwoods on silvery nights,
each step a chime
of Mercury's moondipped bells,
lighting up tops of tall trees
& phone poles, let oh let
my long worn legs
carry me, let them flash
ribbons of pain if need be,
let them hum & keep on
humming along
these hard scarred never-failing
traintracks for the shoes, let
my macerated mind sing,
however shot & torn its notes,
I hope in some known key, let me
break into song like a stand-in Sinatra,
slim & keen in memory

on a crosswalk of teeming ruckus,
I will count on New Yorkers
to ignore me as I croon
unheard-till-now lullabies
to the hysterically worried ghosts
of my parents & grandparents,
not to mention guarders of gates,
keepers of the eternal gasflame,
& all other lost-boss bonus-bribed shades
who haunt electric outlets, for our sakes,
they say, not theirs, it's a hard hard life,
they must at all costs control
rents, royalties, contracts, options,
ad-space & other people's pensions,
as they limousine by, blinded
by their shaded windows, jet
to secret bank Bahamas
& drop to earth on silken parachutes,
landing in jail-less offshore inlets
but never escaping ah the heavy
burdens we will never know,
uneasy the ass that sits upon
the cushion of command,

even if supposedly
safe on the pseudo-farm near
the copter pad, the screening room
and the human layers so useful
for news-filtration & massage!
—Unless & until the green sea opens
& swallows their noise & dust,
dissolving them & emitting
no toxins, coral their bones are
as Egypt's army & the eyes
of Ozymandias! Until that day,
the moving pixels write their claim
across the haze they call the sky
though the scoreboard's gone glazed,
hacked with flickering snow,
the ashes that once were names
fall from the sky as the moving finger,
having writ, moves on.
... As we now know,
all topless towers topple,
soon or late, if not
from age & rot, the weight
of entitlement compounded

with hate... but still,
before the game is over let us stand,
& sing, as I hope to do
even staggering
across the outfield grass,
my eye on the high fly ball
I circle under, lost
in the lights, then not,
hoping for a lucky catch
on a clear day, I sing *I
got it, I got it, I dig it all
the wheel the fold the yolk within yolk
and I promise
even in dreams to remember
and to tell the truth to the best
of my motility
only*
if you want me
come get me, come cut
that cord that
got to fray someday,
right here, right now,
on Church with the Chicken,

who won't look won't bat
an eye at me or anyone,
count on it, like Bartleby
on the Battery, we
may not come when called,
but you can always find me, friend,
I linger in the blue shade
of the long gone Custom House
by the lordly Hudson,
where Herman hid & almost
broke unseen unread ten minutes
by shoe from where I stand
in fumes of dusk with
the long gone ghost
of the costumed birdman.

My dinner's cooked now,
my playmates called & gone,
the streetlights drone metallic buzz
like high power lines unreeling
on steel towers across

snowed-in prairies as far
as memory can see, warning me,
remember: you're a child still
for good or ill, you can't
not get hungry, nor fail to eat
what's on your plate if
you hope to keep on
trucking, in what's left
& what's yet to come
in the number one big city!
For this day at least, the day
of my once-in-a-lifetime
chicken sighting, I've done
enough, and muffled I sink I melt
in a lull
of bone weariness
on the wine-dark darkening brick
& brownstone sea, &
seeing the shore, I say,
OK, I'll go then, go
if I must indoors, just let
me take one more breath
between now & then,

& in that breath
I'll fucking step out anywhere,
up Varick down
Broadway, as high
or low as the way
I feel, feeling sure
that as the step wanders
let the mind rejoice, the mind
in space turn easy cartwheels
bathed in golddust slanting sunbeams
of soft encrusted city air,
no need now anymore
to care who
spots me who
grabs my eye or
pulls my coat my
thinning hair who
tells me what
words to wear what
not to say or see
where not to stare.

APPARITION

(for C.C. Ryder)

When the night wind blew,
my wife came like a child,
straw hair cut short,
nape of neck pale
in backyard moonlight,
to soothe the wildly flapping
bellowing beach umbrella.
She slipped underneath
to release him,
the wind whipping all about them,
as he subsided
under her hand.

A DAY'S WORK

Picasso kept painting
over and over, going
from a movie theatre
where people sit in chairs
and a beam of light
crosses above them,
while an usherette stands
outside in a street
which rolls like a ribbon,
past a house of flexing,
changing walls, which vanishes,
to the sea, to a beach, alive
with sails & swimmers
floating, dividing, drowning
in a sudden flood of shade,
the beam now the rope
of a water skier pulled
into the sky, while the top
of the theatre is an awning,

beneath which people sit
at tiny tables overlooking
the sea, and in two strokes
a man appears who boldly
stands behind the woman
and grows as she grows,
with her arm up then down,
her head turning left, turning
right, turning into hair
on a huger head, her breasts
now colossal, classic, held
at once from three angles
as the man fits closer,
absorbed in her then apart,
the two shimmering in
syncopated givings & takings,
oscillating on the edge of
finality, he might think, but
they burst like tropical flowers
into another incarnation,
while the background flashes
behind them, their clothes

come and go, the two of them
flare and fuse and flicker
as the layers fly on, the moon
rises and falls, stars shoot
by and fall away, the painter not
stopping at any of the many
moments when the painting
is good, I've ruined it, he murmurs,
not caring or pausing even
in obliteration, letting it throb
and roll in a tide of ceaseless
re-creation, laying on
sheets and curls of paint,
pasting in scraps of paper
cutting out and pasting
and dabbing and dotting and
painting the paper, covering
the canvas in full brush sweeps
exact and defined as the finest
tautest line, down which
he plunges, reaching for the shape
of his discovery, not reshaping,

simply & swiftly releasing it,
timing its molecular roll,
catching it, painting it, letting in
light more light the clarity
that begins in dark and ends
in quiet night, a cooling
of the sand and a calmness
settling the waters, a still
in the night sky, until all
that was there all along
consumes more than the space
and time he could have
known he had, until all he had
is played out into it,
and he has exhausted
all that had come and gone
and it is done and
could not be more done.
He steps back then, his eyes
flare & fix, then cool.
He looks away, he shrugs, not
satisfied but finished for now,

having reached the point where
he can rise like the sun
the next morning, knowing
where he will start.

What he has left is simpler.
Shapes loom against the form
of street and beach and sky.
The man and woman are swept
together, their limbs folded,
turning in a delicate dance
which does not hold still.

FORTUNE COOKIE

When others talk,
the wise man appears
to listen. You will
meet your true love,
but you won't know her.
Your car has been stolen.
The water is running
in your tub. Soon
you will go to a party,
and be sorry. When you
go to the restroom,
the others at your table
make fun of you.
Now is the time to
undertake great tasks,
but what are they?
Chinese people find you
an ill-mannered lout.
No need to worry, all

difficulties iron out
in laundry, now or later,
lost or found or after owner
moves or dies, no matter.
No ticket no wash but
wise man doesn't mind.
Wisdom arrives too late,
store closed, work done,
sun low, bus gone, but
you enjoy anyhow,
you better off.

KAFKA TO FELICE

Dearest, You once said
you would like to sit
beside me as I write.
I can barely write anyway,
but in that case I
could not write at all.
Don't you know
that writing means
surrender to the depths
of the self, which,
outside, among people,
would mean a loss of self,
from which anyone
in his right mind would
shrink as one shrinks
from death.
When one writes
from the surface, when

the deeper wells are covered
and lost—the writing is nothing,
and one stumbles in dread
until that moment
a true feeling comes, and all
collapses. One falls alone
into the abyss, and only
alone can one hope
to return. One
can never be
alone enough
when one writes,
there can never be enough
silence around one
when one writes, why
even night is not
night enough.

II.

And then there is
never enough time,
for the roads are long and it is easy
to lose one's way,

and there are times
one is taken by fear and starts
to scurry back—a false move
always punished later. But
how much more so
if one were to receive
a sudden kiss
from beloved lips!

III.

I have thought the best life
for me would be to sit
in the innermost room
of a spacious locked cellar
with my pen and paper and one lamp.
Food would be put down far away,
outside the outermost door.
The walk to my food, in my robe,
through the echoing empty vaults,
my only exercise.
At my table I would eat
slowly and deliberately
—and then

start writing again
at once. At last
I would write!
From what depths
I would drag it up!
Without effort!
Pure concentration
knows no effort.
But could I keep it up?
The first failure—and even
in ideal surroundings sooner
or later I could not avoid it—
would end in a fit
of grandiose madness.

IV.

Well, dearest,
what do you think?
Don't hold back with...
your cellar-dweller, Franz.

adapted from the Stern-Duckworth translation

LEAR WOWS POPS

A heavyweight
father jumped
on stage, grabbed
old Lear and said,
—Hey Kingy, you
ask that girl
too much you
end up more
sinned against
than sinning!

A weepy Dad
cried, take it
from me, Chops!
You let her
go love others,
she love you
till you croak!

After Lear's fall,
these grand daddies
limped dry-eyed
in the cool night air.
I tried, one said,
to warn him.
Some folk's children,
said the other,
never learn,
and see, just
see what happen.
Yeah, they said,
and yeah, and
gimped on home
in speechless
satisfaction.

COUNT BASIE & OSCAR PETERSON

Where else, brother,
in your blessed life
will you hear
two souls
rich with years
swing to such
perfection?

Coming in
with gentle greetings
—you first—no you,
they take care
never to step
on the other's
fat little
deadly fingers.

So totally
respectfully
together,

the execution
inextricable
from anticipation,
the easy shock
of entry, sharing
wild libraries
of ingrown space,
one crunching chords
like sanskrit
punctuation,
while his partner strides
the board easy
as a midnight thief,
in fingertip tiptoe
runs extended
beyond the end of where
they could ever be,
emerging without effort
to 8-bar trades
of tasty flights
of wit.

Soon they
swing outside, singing,
calling, stomping,
with hardly
a sweat, salted
with sweet
filigrees
of wild high
piano grace.
Keening, comping,
interjecting
more outrageous
mellow drolleries
in the twist
of a single
note.

They shake
your mood like fresh
cool bedding,

as with each shift
you inwardly
laugh for glee,
in a way
you'd forgot
you could
ever be.

These old round
black guys get
the music from
the old well lost
and grown over,
way back down
by the river, along
the railroad tracks
where the midnight special
moans and wails
around the bend,
the train that cannot stop
or miss a beat but yes

it's still a-coming, believe
your ears!—bringing
the long gone
trouble tales like
water to
bone dry
desert ramblers.

Choosing
without losing, always
in touch,
never
too much,
blowing the top
off where
you thought
a song must stop.
Light as breath
deep as pain, calm
as rippling light,
which never fades ...

way back where
I can find you,
after you've gone
after you've gone away.

FIRE

In the night
a fire came.
She sat up
red with flame.
You brought this
on, she said,
you are to blame.
Wild wild wild wild
I grabbed a spark,
flew out the window,
and into the dark.

AFTERSHOCK

Then, just then—in cars sliding
across the surface of
what once more turns out to be
the skin of an enormous egg—
with infinite curve but
no thickness, cracking
to let sudden
fingers of shock rumble through,
rip up the freeway,
shake it loose like bedsheets
and yank it out
from under, letting
the mighty double-decked concrete barrel of
the Cypress Overpass of U.S. Eight-Eighty
collapse like
an anchorman's ego—
did those doomed & diving drivers
in that thin millisecond
their last and only chance to

think think
Ah, here comes just what
I always thought?

———

—As when exactly
at the wrong time one hears
I love you,
and shakes one's goofy head
to clear that blinding
flash of pain.

———

When no word came
from my younger son because
no one when it counts
can ever reach
the nub of the root
of the seed of the pitch of the gist
of the crux of the core

of the epicenter,
I saw him dead, though
yes I knew,
as any fool knows walking
the street day by day,
the magnitude
of near-certainty
of his temporary survival.

―――――――

Yet I went about
un-lighting & re-lighting
the pilot light, picking
up downed objects,
saving the save-worthy,
tossing the non-worthy,
until once more
I heard his beloved voice, which,
even then I knew
had a number I couldn't know
attached to it: the Xth time

in a series of Y
the sound of his music
will reach my ear.

———————

Ah then, let me
hear you well, my son,
let us revel
in all that is said and unsaid
as we roll on down
the speckled freckled rippling roadway
we assume behind
and before us.

———————

On quake day, the landscape parts
serenely before me,
as my car cuts its infallible groove
through the twinings of rolling
objects and dwindling lanes

into a snug berth at
the toll booth where a hand
reaches symmetrically
to my hand
takes my ticket and makes
the daily deal for safe passage.
I pull away, my revved-up
engine smoothly levels, clear
jazz soothes my brain,
in control at least
of the radio,
I lift up into the blue
and across the Bay Bridge,
cleverly, illegally
pulling out
into the bus
& carpool lane,
speeding by masses
of cars and trucks
and vision-blocking vans,
waiting like lumpish metal sheep
as I drive on,

my vision focused
as an exit lane, not sensing
a belch of stale breath which
even then wafts
from the roadbed below, where
the chain of metal molecules
begins to snap and dance,
as I sail alone,
encapsulated and propelled
on a pre-set course within
infinite eggs of hidden
pre-set courses,
if only I should know it,
in this world our lie.

Five minutes later
in his cozy highrise study,
my friend glances mildly startled,
as the floor begins to leap,
the walls ramble

and our eyes meet as infants'
in dumb questioning, unable
to believe this is it until
this is no longer it, while
on the bridge I just now left behind me,
a flap
of deck hinges down,
opening a hole,
a ramp to elsewhere,
down which a driver sails
like Alice approaching
the bulging sea.
My friend & I unable
to imagine this or even
not to giggle
at our fear, our silly blips
of panic, still, who knows? we're up,
and lurching about we brace
in adjacent doorways
while the building rattles and shears
whips centrifugally
about our heads.

I see the older man hunch
his shoulders as if to take
the weight of what
may come from above—
though in a moment
he smiles
at the sight of us still
standing there. Releasing the walls
we wait through afterheavings,
or, for all we know,
the end of the beginning
of no more nothing,
and begin to talk, why not, I spin
for him a dream, no longer
exactly the past night's dream,
jumbled now beyond recall,
but a snatch of the wild moment,
the dream of dreams
pushing up,
years in the budding
beneath the topsoil
of one's customary skull like

an ancient burial mound,
full of the previously possible
as real as a century's overgrowth
of domesticated lawn grass,
a dream in which
I see I
can take my terror and shape it
like a bridge
between
what I've known
and what amazing thing I
yet may make,
which begins then
to shake loose inside me,
with nothing to stop
it now, unless
the earth untimely opens,
and I slip
inside.

The city heaves
and gasps around us,
like an old man choking, subsides
once more and my friend and I
now part to find what parts
of our outside selves remain
and scoop them up and put them
in order, hold them
fast against the next spasm.
I find myself driving, driving
yet once more
in that selfsame driver's seat my ass
in all its ages comes back to,
through black topped streets,
where cars bow and wait
at the emptied sockets
of dead stop lights, past
corners adorned with
king-for-a-night traffic directors,
I arrive at Spike's
cellar gallery packed

with pictures, masks, spears, vases strewn
and thrown in disarray
into every open inch.
Spike looks up wild-eyed
from where he stoops
crunching among jumbled pieces
raging at his partner,
his ex-girl who will no longer—
why should she, why
the hell should she?—
dash to the corner
for candles and more whiskey
till his dealer comes. OK,
he grabs back
the twenty he pressed
into her hand, and she flounces off
to wander the blacked-out city,
make bandages, soothe the shaken
and dance all night.

Down the street,
my friend Noelle on the first evening
of her new pill she hopes will span
the gulf of panic
that gapes in her mind
and let her safely cross
the hours of her days,
is terrified
to face what she will find
climbing the stairs
to her third-floor bay-window
one-room office,
where she's written three meticulous
scholarly books, ensconced
behind a lace Dutch curtain
overlooking Haight Street,
and pondering a corner of Europe
where troubador song began.
Her hand shaking on its own now,
I must take the key
and open her neat clean door,

solid as ever,
behind which she finds
the precious pieces of her life,
the ancient books, the notes, the little cups
and long-ago postcards
from poets in Paris shredded
in the insane
randomness of rubble.
Not knowing what to do I stand
holding her in the fragrant heat
of her large worried body.
With my free hand I
press the buttons, hand her the phone,
her husband at home far out
on the avenues, wakened,
answers with a yawn, what quake,
he says, come home.

Dawn sits on a bench with me
in the wooded heights
of Presidio Park

watching a plumed funnel
of smoke rise down by the Bay
from a landfill prairie
of single stucco houses, where
old people live and rich people
keep their yacht club staffed
by uniformed servants, emblem
of imagined old nobility
—as upscale singles meet
at the Safeway Wednesday nights
and modern women liberate
their breasts to the sun
as they lie on the dog-stained grass.
Dawn whom I hardly know I know
takes me in and feeds me
thawed food from her depowered
refrigerator and we lie
on the floor
with candles listening
to the radio while her son Jonesy
says he's going out
on his skateboard and away he rolls—
straight to the flames—

shoving downhill on Divisidero,
his bandanna tucked tight
locking his sculptured shock
of hair to his shaved neck—waving
to his mom with a bug-off thrust,
to say, it's long past time,
I'm gone now, nothing
to discuss, no use
for years of warnings,
sure I'm coming back,
and if not, my ass
is mine.

Dawn takes my arm as
we walk through the spookily
warm & torpid night
of earthquake season,
hot little blasts of air
around our feet like puppies
along the lake where people
afraid to get caught again indoors

stand speechlessly
shaking over bonfires,
while others, their opposites,
watch from darkened windows,
afraid to step out in the open.
Dawn and I find shelter
in a hollow bandshell,
emptied of summer's music,
where we lean
precariously
against one another,
not knowing yet how to fit,
watching the moon beyond Land's End
tugging at the sea, pulling
subtly on the Pacific land plate
as Dawn's thigh pulses
beneath my fluttery hand
and the park falls silent
as a stone, what is this, where
has the wind gone the cooing
of night birds,
the tiny rustlings we
never knew we heard?

On the pull-out bed
in her back room we loll
on one another
like newborn kittens,
fresh and squirming
with the oddness of it all, but
with not a clue
as to what's happening anywhere, only
for us at least
how can we help it,
tonight is a first, a Passover, different
from all other nights, but
God of Israel her panties,
through no one's fault and much,
one might say,
to her credit, are riveted
tighter than the coiled wire
unraveling
in the pillars of
the Admiral Nimitz Expressway.
On this night when all gives way

Dawn's pants will stand
in place, a still point
in my wanderings,
a fact like a breast on which
I rest my head, and
next thing I know
it's morning, and she says, Jeremy,
when you snored I
could have killed you!
So good she says it instead
of doing it, the curse is off,
her son sweetly sleeping
in his bed where
we never heard him come,
and as we gaze on the child's face
he wears in sleep only,
I am full of joy for her relief,
and wordlessly we know
the seal between us now is
broken, as though
we've lived through
natural disasters
since Nineteen-Six.

Hand in hand, we venture out
into the semi-ravaged streets
to buy breakfast, that
most married of meals,
a cup of burnt seven-eleven coffee and
a fresh hot loaf of corn rye
waiting baked for us
and handed out free
by the bakery because
hear ye the earth has risen
like the strip that parted
the Red Sea and once more bread
cannot be delivered.

I drive the long way round
the Bay, across two scarcely
oscillating bridges, arriving home
to find the clocks stopped at five-oh-five,
the power off, and one
baffled dog determined to spend

the rest of her life
beneath my feet. My ex-wife
calls from Ottawa,
her voice low and hard with fear,
having been phoned by one son only
and seen on TV—
while Dawn and I sat in the park—
sixty cars crunched
in a freeway sandwich
quick and solid as the grave—
filling her with dread
for the son unheard-from
and unreachable, in Santa Cruz
where the downtown mall imploded,
rocks and mud
ripped down from on high,
and customers screamed
for their favorite waitress vanished
in the back room
of a doughnut shop, refusing
to believe she had either
dodged out or perished,

wanting her to go on being there,
as much a part of them
as the hole
in their daily doughnut.

My cool boy, as I learn
one long day later, lounged
in his classroom as snowflakes
of fluorescent glass
sprinkled from the ceiling,
idly amused to see
his colliding classmates jam the dooway
and trample the fallen
in their rush for the outside.
He strolled the trails of the crumpled
campus, noting the waste
of pompous orders yelled amid
other odd & useless reactions,
found a friend's room
and settled in to watch

the upheaval on TV,
in the center of the center
of where it all came down.

———————

He saw the tight faced tight
fisted lean mean Governor prowl
down wasted streets, surrounded
by press and musing
if public money perhaps
should be spent on the public. Next
in the hot pale light
came the virgin Vice
President, in V-necked sweater
and flight jacket, slurring
the words his tutors
taught him to say
as he flew on his special plane
along the coast from L.A.,
seeking to soothe
the possibly voting faces

whom he and his co-conspirators
had promised not to tax
to sustain the structure
of life as we know it,
glowing in comfort
from the tube.

———

Having picked up my pieces,
straightened my house,
listened at last
to the longed-for voice
of my no-longer-missing
insouciant son,
I sleep ten hours, get up
and pronounce myself
officially All Right,
ready to receive
concerned phone calls
from all the round world,
which thinks we've been flattened
in lava like Pompeii.

But in the middle
of my morning's work,
my body starts to tremble,
as if the air around me still
gapes and quakes and something
inside me instead
of holding firm gives way
and curling down inside
the marrow of my bones
time itself is shaking,
time which I always
prefer to ignore, but
in my bones
it's shaking-time,
and on the hour I shake.

And soon I hear
the oh-so-serious California
voices telling
how they felt
at one with the earth,

and No, I say, let
the earth be,
I'm willing enough
to walk my walk and talk
my talk upon
its still-spherical pod, but once
it has yawned and yawped,
warped and warbled under
my lifelong trusting self my
sack of blood and bones,
I cannot expel
the grain of thought
that one day
it will open its mouth again
just for me. Till then,
if I can
keep on, just make my noise,
that last great groan may never come,
or wait at least till I am done, so
why not keep trucking then,
banal as it is but better,
never say die, or
at least not lie

when I say
to those I love,
I will not take
my heart away
from yours or break
what bonds I make even
in my dreams. Each time I wake
I croak
and am consecrated
in each morning's grief,
each morning's toast,
and am relieved
when morning brings
one whole song one
rare embrace.
At least at last when I
slide away, let me wake
with a jolt see where I am
shout strike run make
Death reach hard to grab me.
I will not drive down
who knows what last street
with smarmy simplicities

of tunnel vision
or empty pie-faced waves
or moon-smiles.

———

My boyhood friend Frank,
who walks with a cane
against the pain of wrenched bones, looked
up from the book
on Norse Gods
he studied on his handbuilt couch
in the glass and redwood
mini-fort he put together
beam by joist
in his youth,
high on the peak of the ridge
twelve miles above
the churning depths where
the grinding plates of earth
wrenched clockwise,
and saw his cat leap madly
ten times in the air.

As his fireplace tumbled,
as the levels
of his sunken floor changed
places, he heard a wall fall
over and the house begin
to shuffle in around him
like a deck of cards.
Now Frank knew
he should get to a doorframe, but
he knew too the current state
of his legs would force him down
to creep on all fours,
or slide like a splayed frog,
so he sat
in the center of the pit
with the cat in his lap
and rode it out, damned
if he would be more
damned than always, and thinking,
go ahead You,
take me,
if you want me,
I'm not going to crawl.

SOCIAL CONTRACT

The mask of Phumbu,
the executioner,
looks the same as
the mask of Fumu,
the chief, except for
Phumbu's blood red feather.
Yet the difference
is clear, as all who
know know clear must be.
At the circumcision dance,
Phumbu lunges
with his knife, while
Fumu moves about
sedately, a fly-whisk
in hand, a parasol
held above him, as befits
a chief born only
to give commands—or so
we watchers all agree,
and without us,

how could there be
parts to play, or masks,
ceremonies,
feast days, crownings,
slicings, killings,
or dances for us
to see? How then
could we be we?

READING LESSON
(for the official TV poet)

goshgolly you
wrote a neat poem
to suit the kit
of schoolkids,
now say it
trippingly
as if fit
for a rapt, attentive whippet,
do not intone the poem
nor clip it,
as if to hammer words
onto your tombstone—
you exist,
however slightly,
like anyone, speak
lightly,
in a voice
that could be true.
between us two,
the poem's the thing,
not you.

KEATS FOR HOME & FAMILY

Duty is proof, proof duty:
That is all ye know
In hell, and even that
Ye don't know very well.

A BREED YOU'LL NEVER BE

A dog
moves sideways
like a snake,
up and down
like a lion,
nose to the ground/tail to the wind
like a politician,
and occasionally
will eat shit,
not to get on
in the world,
but just because
it's there.

THE ROAD NOT TAKEN

(for Zack)

I have some advice
the father said,

about going
your own way.

Wait! Where
are you going?

LONG BIG DAISYBUSH DREAMSNAP

So much too much
Eyescreaming precious pretty
Daisy blazing
Wakeupshock!
No may gather
Should we may!
Wipe eye, rash gazer
Look away!
Blond sunny dawnshiners
Skyhoggers
Petalheaded mellow mugs
Eggyolkynoddyhappy
Halo-peteled nitwit zombies
Junglegreen leaflolly rot-gut
Starpox beauty
Sideways dreaming
Hip-hill shoulder-swelling
Rubadub rib dip
Belly valley

Tinyhead
Hedgeblock noseblowing
Morning flyaway
Roll over, clover
Gotta get outta
Crazy to piss
Be on my way,
Seize he mutter
Fucking day!

BIG ROOSTER BLUES

Come ruffle
my feathers
with your hard
little beak.
Give the grizzle-gizzard,
wattle-mottled,
scarred game heart
a tweak.
Pluck me, baby,
till I hear
your neck bone
squeak. My meat's
tough & tender,
let's tread it
long & slow,
& in the A.M.,
you can catch
this old cock crow.

JEREMY LARNER grew up in Indiana, went to New York City at 22, and stayed there throughout the 1960s, writing five books in that period. His first novel, *Drive, He Said*, won the Delta Prize and became an underground classic. As a freelance journalist, Jeremy published articles, essays and stories in many magazines, including *Harpers*, *The Paris Review*, and *Life*, for which he covered the Mexico City Olympics. In  1968, he became a principal speechwriter for Eugene McCarthy's presidential campaign, and afterwards wrote a book, *Nobody Knows*, about that experience.

In 1971, *Drive, He Said* was made into a movie (directed by Jack Nicholson, who collaborated with Jeremy on the screenplay). In 1973, Jeremy got an Oscar for Best Original Screenplay for his script of *The Candidate*.

In 1987, Jeremy began to write poetry, and the tremendous response to his readings prompted inclusion of a CD in this, his first collection of poems. In 1992, Jeremy moved back to New York City, where he was inspired to write "Chicken on Church." He now lives outside of San Francisco, writing poetry, working on his Hollywood novel, and making notes for his memoirs.